# WELCOME TO GALAXY

# EARTH

I am the planet you live on. I am the only planet with organic life. I am 4.5 billion years old. I complete one rotation around my own axis in 23 hours 58 minutes and 4 seconds .

My Name Is SUN

# SUN

I am star not a planet.
I was found at the center
of the Solar System. I make 99.86%
of the Solar System masse.
My Light reaches you in around
8 minutes.

# My Name Is MERCURY

# MERCURY

I am the closest planet to the sun.

A year on my surface is 88 days.

I am the smallest planet in the Sollar System.

I don't have any satellites or ring systems.

My Name Is VENUS

# VENUS

I am the hottest planet in the Sollar System. I am the brightest. I have an active surface including volcanoes. I spin the opposite direction of Earth.

My Name Is MARS

# MARS

I am red in color. I am the fourth planet from the sun. I have the highest mountain in the Solar System and a volcano named Olympus Mons.

My Name Is JUPITER

# JUPITER

I am covered in clouds and I am the fivest from the sun.
I am the largest planet in the Solar System.
My giant red spot is a raging storm.

# SATURN

I am brown in color. My outer rings are extremely thin. They are made of dust and icy chunks.

I am the King of the Moons, having a total of 82 confirmed moons.

My Name Is URANUS

# URANUS

I am blue in color. Humans have named me the icy planet. I am the coldest planet in the Solar System.
It is possible to see me with the naked eye.

My Name Is NEPTUNE

# NEPTUNE

I am blue in color just like URANUS. I have too many storms in my atmosphere. I am the furthest planet from the sun.

# WE HOPE YOU ENJOYED IT

www.ingramcontent.com/pod-product-compliance
Lightning Source LLC
Chambersburg PA
CBHW081630100526
44590CB00021B/3673